30 DAY CHAMPIONS JOURNAL

An Edge in Sports, Habits for Life

Priscilla Tallman · Joe Jardine

30 Day Champions Journal

(originally titled 30 Day Reset Journal)

Priscilla Tallman & Joe Jardine

ISBN 13: 978-1-954437-64-7

Journal design by Esther BeLer Wodrich. www.estherbeler.com

To my parents, Mary and Joe, for endless support during my playing days and to my husband, Rich, and our children, Joaquin and Lyncoln, who support and value my work as a coach.

–Priscilla

For my wife, Kristin and our children Sawyer and Avonlea. You cannot reset your mindset without family.

–Joe

30 Days of Mental Training for WHOLE Athletes

Welcome athlete! We are excited for you to join the team journaling movement with our **30 Day Champions Journal**. WHOLE athletes are people who train their body, mind and emotions in order to perform at the highest levels on and off the playing arena.

In case you didn't already know, journaling is a powerful mindset tool. Research in this area supports that journaling not only helps clarify your thoughts and feelings by writing them out, it can help reduce cortisol levels (the stress hormone), lead to more effective problem solving skills, resolve conflicts and promote healthy forms of communication with others such as those found in team environments.

This journal contains 30 days of prompts and daily routines used by our professional and collegiate athletes to make them mentally elite in their sport. We believe by investing ten minutes each day on your mindset, journaling can help train your mind and develop the habits you need to get a competitive edge in your sport and give you valuable life skill too.

Priscilla Tallman
NCAA Performance Mindset Coach

Joe Jardine
NCAA/NFL Performance Mindset Coach

GETTING **STARTED**

Your **30 Day Champions Journal** contains a Pre-Game Huddle, 28 days of journal pages, and a Post-Game Huddle for a total of 30 days. The seventh day of each week ends with a **RECAP**. After the completion of week 4 you will be prompted to complete the Post-Game Huddle.

The **Pre and Post-Game Huddle** are assessments that will measure your mindset growth throughout the 30 days. Before starting "Day 1", fill out the Pre-Game Huddle assessment. Be as honest as you can. If you don't understand a question, leave it blank or guess what you think it might mean and enter your score. After "Day 28", complete the Post-Game Huddle assessment at the end of the journal. Compare the first assessment to the second one and see if there are improvements or areas in which you feel you have grown. Are there certain areas in which you would like to do more work? Is there anything that stayed the same or where no growth occurred? Tracking these areas may help you to become more self-aware of your process and own the parts where more work is needed.

A daily routine is very important in the development of your performance mindset. Routine primes confidence and success. *Routine re-sets the mind-set.* For the rest of your career, develop a routine on how you approach practices and the game. Set it and stick with it.

Each day contains a **DAILY RESET** with three components to be completed before your journal prompt.

Practicing your daily reset will help begin to shift your mind from the negative to the positive. You are training your brain to look at the strengths and not the deficits of yourself as an athlete.

1: **Self-Evaluation** — Learning how to accurately and honestly assess our emotions on any given day is a valuable life skill that creates self-awareness. Each day, start by identifying your emotional state. If you score less than a 6, it is encouraged you share that with a coach or healthy adult.

2: **3-2-1 Journaling** — We have to train our minds to begin each day from a place of abundance and gratitude. Gratitude creates an emotional shift from the inside out, but it takes daily practice to see things we may otherwise overlook.

3: **Visualization** — rehearsing a great practice or acquisition of skill is a great tool to making it happen and minimize anxiety in the moment.

TABLE OF CONTENTS

PRE-GAME HUDDLE

____ / ____ / ____

Rate yourself for each question below using this scale:

1	2	3	4	5
needs work	*meh*	*its fine*	*good*	*great!*

Rate your attitude as an athlete. ________

Rate your effort as an athlete. ________

Rate your openness to feedback. ________

Rate your application of feedback. ________

Rate your openness to ask questions. ________

Rate your pre-practice physical preparation. ________

Rate your pre-game physical preparation. ________

Rate your pre-practice mental preparation. ________

Rate your pre-game mental preparation. ________

Rate your openness to learn something new. ________

Rate your overall performance as an athlete. ________

developing your

MINDSET

Where is your brain?
That's right, it's inside your head.

Where are your muscles?
That's right, they're inside your body.

Some athletes make the mistake and think that mindset or mental work is done separately from the physical aspects of your sport, but your body and mind work together they are literally in the same space - therefore mindset work IS your sport.

Answer these questions: *What type of athlete do you want to be? What daily decisions does that athlete possess? What habits does that athlete possess?* Decisions become habits and habits become systems. In fact, "*we do not rise to the level of our goals, we fall to the level of our systems*" –James Clear, Atomic Habits.

THEREFORE, YOUR MINDSET IS A CHOICE.

When you create healthy daily habits you free up valuable brain power and energy to learn technical aspects of your sport - and that's how you develop your mindset.

DAILY RESET – MINDSET

➡ **Rate Yourself.** On a scale of 1-10
(1 = low mood, hopeless / 10 = great mood)
rate your overall mood today. Emotional self affects your performance, so self awareness in this area is important.

Write your score: ______ / 10

➡ **3-2-1 Journaling**

3 things you are ***grateful for***

____

____

____

2 things you are ***excited about***

____

____

1 thing you want to ***accomplish*** for yourself today

____

➡ **Visualize.** Spend 5 minutes visualizing what you want to accomplish at practice or in your game today. Find a quiet spot, close your eyes and rehearse this intention.

HOW DO I FEEL TODAY? *(circle the emoji(s) that apply)*

This is called *checking in*. You can check in on your own or with a teammate or coach. It's important to know how we show up for practice and what we may be carrying into our training session.

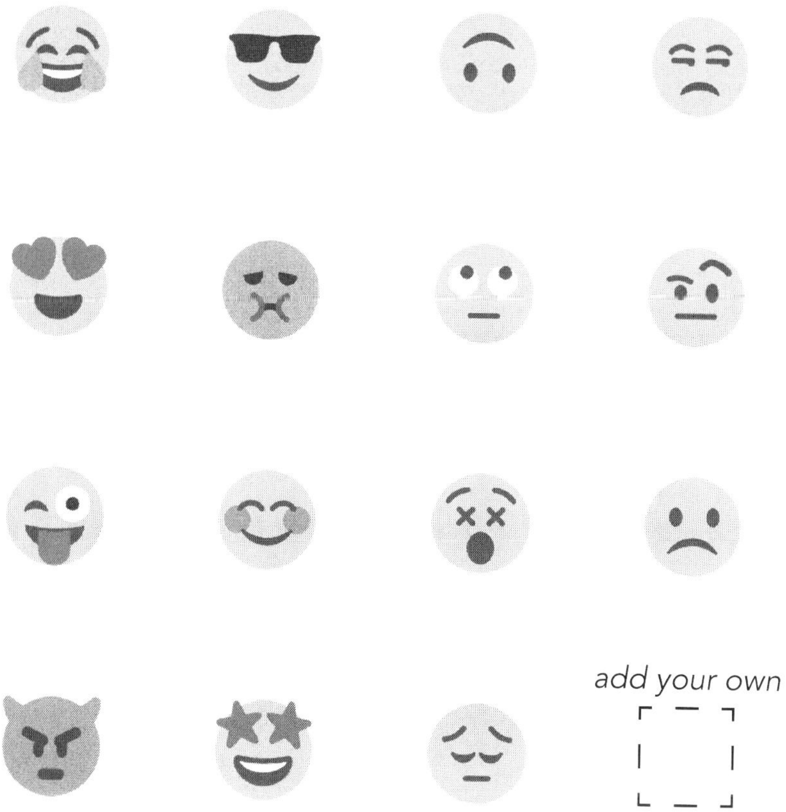

add your own

NEXT LEVEL: *Write the corresponding feeling underneath the emoji(s) you circled.*

DAILY RESET – MINDSET

➡ **Rate Yourself.** On a scale of 1-10
(1 = low mood, hopeless / 10 = great mood)
rate your overall mood today. Emotional self affects your performance, so self awareness in this area is important.

Write your score: ______ / 10

➡ **3-2-1 Journaling**

3 things you are ***grateful for***

____

____

____

2 things you are ***excited about***

____

____

1 thing you want to ***accomplish*** for yourself today

____

➡ **Visualize.** Spend 5 minutes visualizing what you want to accomplish at practice or in your game today. Find a quiet spot, close your eyes and rehearse this intention.

___ / ___ / ___

Our support system, or the people who surround and support us daily, are an important part of our success on and off the field. List below the people who fit that role in your life.

3 ***people who support me***

____

____

____

2 ***people who hold me accountable***

____

____

1 ***person who comforts me when I'm struggling***

____

DAILY RESET – MINDSET

Rate Yourself. On a scale of 1-10
(1 = low mood, hopeless / 10 = great mood)
rate your overall mood today. Emotional self affects your performance, so self awareness in this area is important.

Write your score: ______ / 10

3-2-1 Journaling

3 things you are ***grateful for***

____

____

____

2 things you are ***excited about***

____

____

1 thing you want to ***accomplish*** for yourself today

____

Visualize. Spend 5 minutes visualizing what you want to accomplish at practice or in your game today. Find a quiet spot, close your eyes and rehearse this intention.

DAY **3**

___/___/___

Before we say the words "I feel nervous" or "I feel stressed" our bodies have already alerted us to what it thinks will be a stressful situation. Our body responses include things like getting butterflies, having to use the restroom, sweaty palms or a racing heart. In the blanks below, write down the different ways you prepare for training or competition.

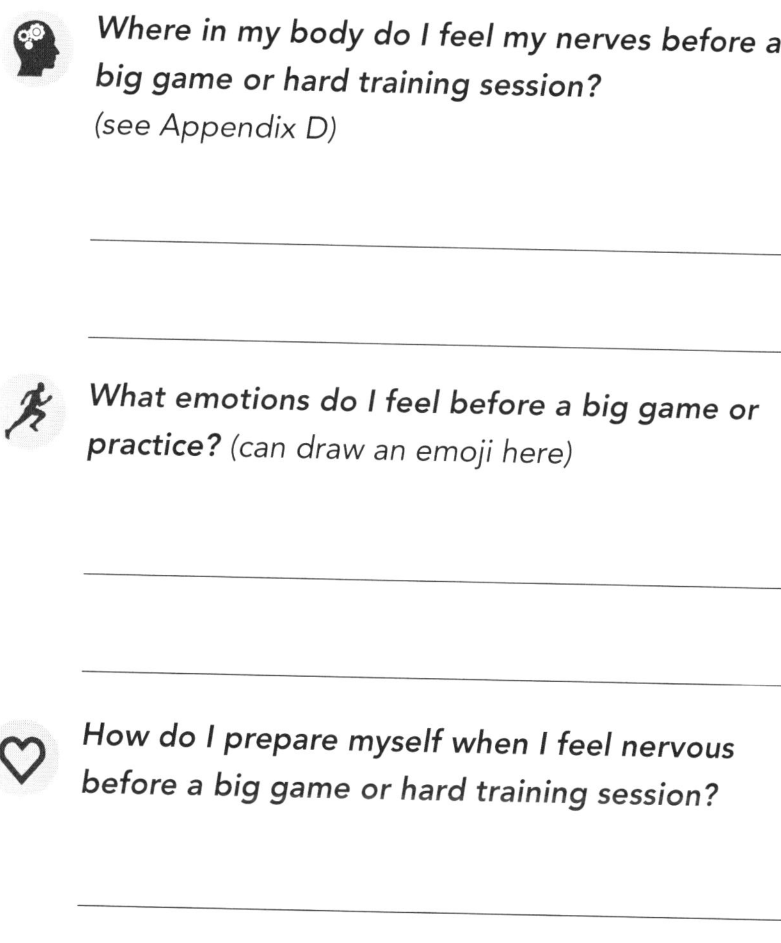

Where in my body do I feel my nerves before a big game or hard training session? *(see Appendix D)*

___

___

What emotions do I feel before a big game or practice? *(can draw an emoji here)*

___

___

How do I prepare myself when I feel nervous before a big game or hard training session?

___

___

SEE APPENDIX **D**

DAILY RESET – MINDSET

➡ **Rate Yourself.** On a scale of 1-10
(1 = low mood, hopeless / 10 = great mood)
rate your overall mood today. Emotional self affects your performance, so self awareness in this area is important.

Write your score: ______ / 10

➡ **3-2-1 Journaling**

3 things you are ***grateful for***

____

____

____

2 things you are ***excited about***

____

____

1 thing you want to ***accomplish*** for yourself today

____

➡ **Visualize.** Spend 5 minutes visualizing what you want to accomplish at practice or in your game today. Find a quiet spot, close your eyes and rehearse this intention.

DAY 4

___ / ___ / ___

"Your results are the product of either personal focus or personal distractions. The choice is yours,"
John Di Lemme

3 **productive activities that lift my mood when I'm down**

____

____

____

2 **productive activities I can do when I feel bored**

____

____

1 **activity I can do to serve/help someone else today**

____

DAILY RESET – MINDSET

➡ **Rate Yourself.** On a scale of 1-10
(1 = low mood, hopeless / 10 = great mood)
rate your overall mood today. Emotional self affects your performance, so self awareness in this area is important.

Write your score: ______ / 10

➡ **3-2-1 Journaling**

3 things you are ***grateful for***

____

____

____

2 things you are ***excited about***

____

____

1 thing you want to ***accomplish*** for yourself today

____

➡ **Visualize.** Spend 5 minutes visualizing what you want to accomplish at practice or in your game today. Find a quiet spot, close your eyes and rehearse this intention.

DAY **5**

___/___/___

It is important for us to know the difference between where we can go to recharge or rest and where we go that distracts us.

3 ***places I can go or things I can do to recharge my energy***

____

____

____

2 ***places I can go to rest***

____

____

1 ***place that is a distraction to me***

____

NEXT LEVEL: *Rest and recovery are important life skills.*

Tear out this page and tape it to a visible place you see every day as a reminder of the ways you can find rest and avoid distractions.

DAILY RESET – MINDSET

➡ **Rate Yourself.** On a scale of 1-10
(1 = low mood, hopeless / 10 = great mood)
rate your overall mood today. Emotional self affects your performance, so self awareness in this area is important.

Write your score: ______ / 10

➡ **3-2-1 Journaling**

3 things you are ***grateful for***

____

____

____

2 things you are ***excited about***

____

____

1 thing you want to ***accomplish*** for yourself today

____

➡ **Visualize.** Spend 5 minutes visualizing what you want to accomplish at practice or in your game today. Find a quiet spot, close your eyes and rehearse this intention.

DAY **6**

___ / ___ / ___

You are almost a week into a new habit! You may have found it easy to get into a routine or it may have been difficult to be consistent. Let's look at what worked for you and what you found challenging.

✓ What worked to keep me consistent with my journal? *(Place a check mark next to each one that helped keep you consistent)*

- ☐ Where I placed my journal each day
- ☐ A coaches check in
- ☐ The time of day I did my journal
- ☐ Having a friend or teammate hold me accountable
- ☐ Setting a timer for when I will do my journal
- ☐ ______________________________

✓ What distracted me or kept me from my journal? *(Place a check mark next to each one that kept you from completing your journal this week)*

- ☐ My phone
- ☐ Friends
- ☐ Social media
- ☐ Sleeping in 5 extra minutes
- ☐ Waiting until too close to bedtime to complete my journal
- ☐ Forgetting to place my journal in a visible place
- ☐ I don't think I need to journal
- ☐ I'm embarrassed to write down what I'm thinking
- ☐ ______________________________

DAILY RESET – MINDSET

Rate Yourself. On a scale of 1-10
(1 = low mood, hopeless / 10 = great mood)
rate your overall mood today. Emotional self affects your performance, so self awareness in this area is important.

Write your score: ______ / 10

3-2-1 Journaling

3 things you are ***grateful for***

____

____

____

2 things you are ***excited about***

____

____

1 thing you want to ***accomplish*** for yourself today

____

Visualize. Spend 5 minutes visualizing what you want to accomplish at practice or in your game today. Find a quiet spot, close your eyes and rehearse this intention.

DAY **7**

___/___/___

RECAP - MINDSET

(circle any that apply or add your own)

What did I **do well** this week?

my attitude
my effort
patience
a certain skill

was a good teammate
open to feedback
good communication
helped setup/teardown
asked good questions

showed up
set practice goals
had manners

____

____

What needs **improving**?

my attitude
my effort
listen to coach
support a teammate

a certain skill
understand rules
understand drill
asking a question

recover from a mistake
reframe a mistake

____

____

What will **I bring** to the next practice or game?

attitude to learn
my best effort
listen to coach
support a teammate

a certain skill
a good question
a practice goal
help setup/teardown

reframe a mistake
be open to feedback
patience
communication

____

____

defining your

GOALS

Goal setting is merely **intention setting.**

As you progress from making decisions that become habits, you now have the foundation to set intentions and those intentions will help you reach your goals.

Goal setting answers these questions:

> *What do I intend to accomplish for this practice?*
>
> *What do we intend to accomplish as a team?*
>
> *How do I intend to contribute my gifts for the good of the team?*

When you set a goal, you have to take it from words on a paper to action steps that get you and your team closer to where you want to be.

DAILY RESET – GOALS

➡ **Rate your sleep, nutrition and physical health** on a scale of 1-10:

1 = little sleep, fast food, junk food, bodily injury or illness

10 = 8+ hours sleep regularly, good food choices and body feels good

Write your score: ______ / 10

➡ **3-2-1 Journaling**

3 great choices *I can make today*

____

____

____

2 ways *I can promote* ***better health***

____

____

1 way *I can keep my body feeling* ***physically prepared*** *for my sport*

____

➡ **Visualize.** Spend 5 minutes visualizing what you want to accomplish at practice or in your game today. Find a quiet spot, close your eyes and rehearse this intention.

DAY 8

___/___/___

Your dreams and goals can be anything. They do not have to be sport related. After all, we are more than athletes and have many aspects of our lives.

Fill the bubble with some

WILD, CRAZY, BIG GOALS

you have.

DAILY RESET – GOALS

Rate your sleep, nutrition and physical health on a scale of 1-10:

1 = little sleep, fast food, junk food, bodily injury or illness

10 = 8+ hours sleep regularly, good food choices and body feels good

Write your score: ______ / 10

3-2-1 Journaling

3 great choices *I can make today*

____

____

____

2 ways *I can promote* ***better health***

____

____

1 way *I can keep my body feeling* ***physically prepared*** *for my sport*

____

Visualize. Spend 5 minutes visualizing what you want to accomplish at practice or in your game today. Find a quiet spot, close your eyes and rehearse this intention.

DAY **9**

___/___/___

Goals rarely make a straight line from point A to point B. **Draw in** what it might look like to set a goal and meet it.

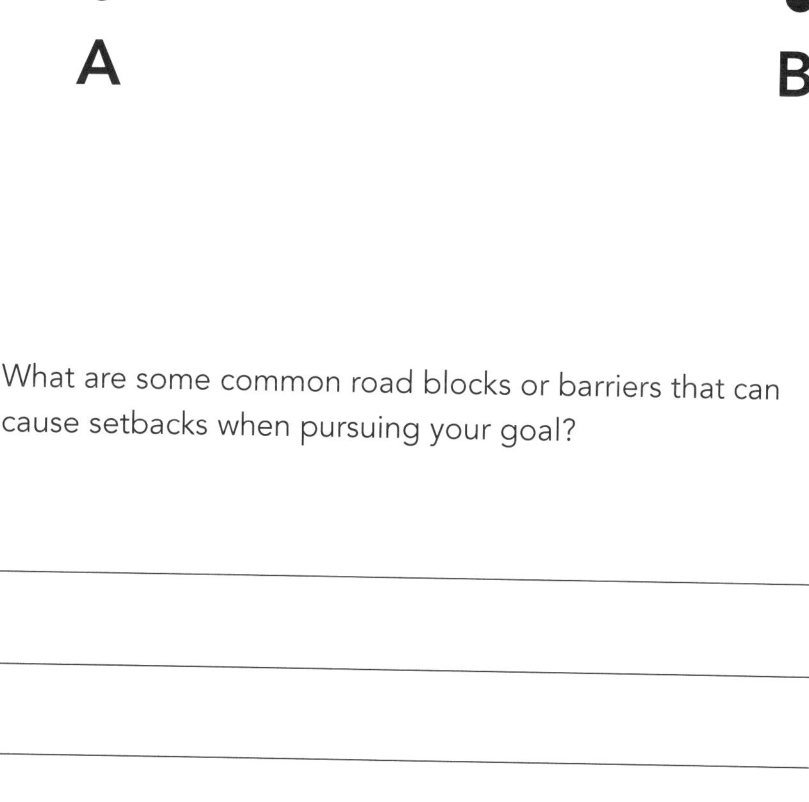

What are some common road blocks or barriers that can cause setbacks when pursuing your goal?

DAILY RESET – GOALS

Rate your sleep, nutrition and physical health on a scale of 1-10:

1 = little sleep, fast food, junk food, bodily injury or illness

10 = 8+ hours sleep regularly, good food choices and body feels good

Write your score: ______ / 10

3-2-1 Journaling

3 great choices *I can make today*

____

____

____

2 ways *I can promote* ***better health***

____

____

1 way *I can keep my body feeling* ***physically prepared*** *for my sport*

____

Visualize. Spend 5 minutes visualizing what you want to accomplish at practice or in your game today. Find a quiet spot, close your eyes and rehearse this intention.

DAY 10

___/___/___

What are some things I feel when my goals seem out of reach? **Circle as many** as you feel appropriate or add your own.

- AFRAID
- ANGRY
- FRUSTRATED
- CLOSED OFF
- ENCOURAGED
- BURNED OUT
- EXHAUSTED
- DISCOURAGED
- MAD
- SAD
- DISAPPOINTED
- LIKE BLAMING SOMEONE
- LIKE I LET SOMEONE DOWN
- DETERMINED
- HOPELESS
- LIKE QUITTING
- PERSISTENT
- RESILIENT
- SICK

____________________ ____________________

____________________ ____________________

Write down your **top three** here.

1. ____________________
2. ____________________
3. ____________________

DAILY RESET – GOALS

Rate your sleep, nutrition and physical health on a scale of 1-10:

1 = little sleep, fast food, junk food, bodily injury or illness

10 = 8+ hours sleep regularly, good food choices and body feels good

Write your score: ______ / 10

3-2-1 Journaling

3 great choices *I can make today*

____

____

____

2 ways *I can promote* ***better health***

____

____

1 way *I can keep my body feeling* ***physically prepared*** *for my sport*

____

Visualize. Spend 5 minutes visualizing what you want to accomplish at practice or in your game today. Find a quiet spot, close your eyes and rehearse this intention.

DAY 11

___/___/___

Think about the first time you shot a layup, served a ball, swung a bat, caught a pop fly or took off from the starting blocks. You didn't get it on your first try did you? No, your coach or a teammate likely broke down the skill into smaller parts. Goals can work that way too.

In the table below, write down one goal and three steps that will help you achieve that goal. Pick something specific and tangible, avoid things like "be better at ..."

Example: Goal = Eat nutritious food that fuels me,
3 Steps = choose a vegetable for one meal, pack a piece of fruit in my bag, choose water instead of soda, juice or energy drinks.

GOAL	3 STEP ACTION PLAN
	1. 2. 3.

NEXT LEVEL: *Pick one goal and complete the 1st step in the 3 step action plan today*

DAILY RESET – GOALS

Rate your sleep, nutrition and physical health on a scale of 1-10:

1 = little sleep, fast food, junk food, bodily injury or illness

10 = 8+ hours sleep regularly, good food choices and body feels good

Write your score: ______ / 10

3-2-1 Journaling

3 great choices *I can make today*

____

____

____

2 ways *I can promote* ***better health***

____

____

1 way *I can keep my body feeling* ***physically prepared*** *for my sport*

____

Visualize. Spend 5 minutes visualizing what you want to accomplish at practice or in your game today. Find a quiet spot, close your eyes and rehearse this intention.

DAY **12**

___ / ___ / ___

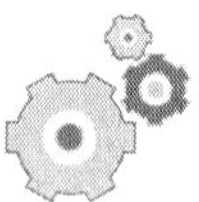

You can only work on **THREE** things at your next practice. What **THREE** things will help you reach one of your personal or team goals?

1. ______________________________

____

2. ______________________________

____

3. ______________________________

____

NEXT LEVEL: *Tell a coach, teammate or family member what you are working on.*

DAILY RESET – GOALS

Rate your sleep, nutrition and physical health on a scale of 1-10:

1 = little sleep, fast food, junk food, bodily injury or illness

10 = 8+ hours sleep regularly, good food choices and body feels good

Write your score: ______ / 10

3-2-1 Journaling

3 great choices *I can make today*

____

____

____

2 ways *I can promote* ***better health***

____

____

1 way *I can keep my body feeling* ***physically prepared*** *for my sport*

____

Visualize. Spend 5 minutes visualizing what you want to accomplish at practice or in your game today. Find a quiet spot, close your eyes and rehearse this intention.

DAY 13

___/___/___

Distractions aren't just things that happen on the field, they are circumstances, conflicts or adversities that can happen at any point in your life. For instance, a tough financial situation in your family can be a distraction. So can academic stress, friend drama, social media, parental conflict, peer pressure and many other things.

What are **THREE** things that might serve as a distraction to your goals?

1. ______________________________

____

2. ______________________________

____

3. ______________________________

____

NEXT LEVEL: *Acknowledging these distractions won't make them go away, but writing them down can help us start the conversation with ourselves and then others. Everyone has distractions, those of us who acknowledge them can learn how to ask for help when we need it.*

DAILY RESET – GOALS

Rate your sleep, nutrition and physical health on a scale of 1-10:

1 = little sleep, fast food, junk food, bodily injury or illness

10 = 8+ hours sleep regularly, good food choices and body feels good

Write your score: ______ / 10

3-2-1 Journaling

3 great choices *I can make today*

____

____

____

2 ways *I can promote* ***better health***

____

____

1 way *I can keep my body feeling* ***physically prepared*** *for my sport*

____

Visualize. Spend 5 minutes visualizing what you want to accomplish at practice or in your game today. Find a quiet spot, close your eyes and rehearse this intention.

DAY **14**

___/___/___

RECAP - GOALS

How did I **work on my mindset** this week?
(e.g. journaling, gratitude, meditating or taking down time)

___

___

___

When is the best time to work on my mental training?

MORNING	BETWEEN CLASSES
BEFORE SCHOOL	AFTER SCHOOL
AFTERNOON	BEFORE BED
BEFORE PRACTICE	AFTER PRACTICE
TRAINING ROOM	OTHER ___

The most helpful part of journaling is:

___

___

___

developing your

com·mu·ni·ca·tion

Your brain has a relationship with words. How you speak to yourself is an important part of shaping your story as an athlete.When the story is off it can get in the way of your performance and limits your ability to hear feedback from your coaches or teammates.

Fear, anxiety, confidence and happiness are influenced by words.

> *The words you say can either be*
>
> **motivating or deflating**
>
> *to you and your teammates.*

One big area we can work on communicating to ourselves or others is looking at how we respond to mistakes or failure.

DAILY RESET – COMMUNICATION

➡ **Rate your self talk** on a scale of 1-10

1 = negative self talk, beating myself up over a mistake or swearing loudly

10 = bouncing back from a mistake, self talk reflects the process, not the result

Write your score: ______ / 10

➡ **3-2-1 Journaling** *(vary your answers for each day)*

3 ways *I can* ***encourage a teammate*** *today*

(pick a different teammate each day this week)

____

____

____

2 ways *I can* ***practice healthy self talk***

(e.g. process oriented vs. result oriented)

____

____

1 helpful thing *I can tell myself before my next practice or game*

____

➡ **Visualize.** Spend 5 minutes visualizing what you want to accomplish at practice or in your game today. Find a quiet spot, close your eyes and rehearse this intention.

DAY **15**

___/___/___

What are some ***healthy ways*** my teammates communicate with me?

1. ____________________

2. ____________________

3. ____________________

What are some ***healthy ways*** I communicate with my teammates and coaches?

1. ____________________

2. ____________________

3. ____________________

DAILY RESET – COMMUNICATION

➡ **Rate your self talk** on a scale of 1-10

1 = negative self talk, beating myself up over a mistake or swearing loudly

10 = bouncing back from a mistake, self talk reflects the process, not the result

Write your score: ______ / 10

➡ **3-2-1 Journaling** *(vary your answers for each day)*

3 ways I can **encourage a teammate** today

(pick a different teammate each day this week)

____

____

____

2 ways I can **practice healthy self talk**

(e.g. process oriented vs. result oriented)

____

____

1 helpful thing I can tell myself before my next practice or game

____

➡ **Visualize.** Spend 5 minutes visualizing what you want to accomplish at practice or in your game today. Find a quiet spot, close your eyes and rehearse this intention.

DAY **16**

___/___/___

Nonverbal communication such as body language, tone or facial expressions can send big messages. List some healthy and not so healthy forms of non-verbal communication.

healthy

not healthy

NEXT LEVEL: *Circle one of the healthy non-verbal communication ways you listed that you want to practice this week. What does it look like in practice? Competition?*

DAILY RESET – COMMUNICATION

➡ **Rate your self talk** on a scale of 1-10

1 = negative self talk, beating myself up over a mistake or swearing loudly

10 = bouncing back from a mistake, self talk reflects the process, not the result

Write your score: ______ / 10

➡ **3-2-1 Journaling** *(vary your answers for each day)*

3 ways *I can* ***encourage a teammate*** *today*

(pick a different teammate each day this week)

____

____

____

2 ways *I can* ***practice healthy self talk***

(e.g. process oriented vs. result oriented)

____

____

1 helpful thing *I can tell myself before my next practice or game*

____

➡ **Visualize.** Spend 5 minutes visualizing what you want to accomplish at practice or in your game today. Find a quiet spot, close your eyes and rehearse this intention.

DAY **17**

___/___/___

Our words matter. What are some healthy and not so healthy ways our coaches or parents communicate with us during competition?

HINT: What kinds of things would you like to hear to feel supported? What kinds of things make you feel discouraged?

healthy

not healthy

DAILY RESET – COMMUNICATION

➡ **Rate your self talk** on a scale of 1-10

1 = negative self talk, beating myself up over a mistake or swearing loudly

10 = bouncing back from a mistake, self talk reflects the process, not the result

Write your score: ______ / 10

➡ **3-2-1 Journaling** *(vary your answers for each day)*

***3 ways** I can **encourage a teammate** today*

(pick a different teammate each day this week)

____

____

____

2 ways** I can **practice healthy self talk

(e.g. process oriented vs. result oriented)

____

____

***1 helpful thing** I can tell myself before my next practice or game*

____

➡ **Visualize.** Spend 5 minutes visualizing what you want to accomplish at practice or in your game today. Find a quiet spot, close your eyes and rehearse this intention.

DAY **18**

___ / ___ / ___

Leadership is revealed by how well you handle your mistakes and the mistakes of others.

Things I **tell a teammate** after they make a mistake.

1. ______________________________

____

____

2. ______________________________

____

____

3. ______________________________

____

____

DAILY RESET – COMMUNICATION

Rate your self talk on a scale of 1-10

1 = negative self talk, beating myself up over a mistake or swearing loudly

10 = bouncing back from a mistake, self talk reflects the process, not the result

Write your score: ______ / 10

3-2-1 Journaling *(vary your answers for each day)*

3 ways *I can* ***encourage a teammate*** *today*

(pick a different teammate each day this week)

____

____

____

2 ways *I can* ***practice healthy self talk***

(e.g. process oriented vs. result oriented)

____

____

1 helpful thing *I can tell myself before my next practice or game*

____

Visualize. Spend 5 minutes visualizing what you want to accomplish at practice or in your game today. Find a quiet spot, close your eyes and rehearse this intention.

DAY 19

___/___/___

Negative self-talk affects our ability to move on quickly from mistakes and reinforces thoughts about performance (e.g. fear, anger, shame).

Things I tell **myself** after a mistake:

1. ______________________________

____

____

2. ______________________________

____

____

3. ______________________________

____

____

NEXT LEVEL: *How does this self-talk differ from how I speak to a teammate? What if I spoke to myself the way I speak to others?*

DAILY RESET – COMMUNICATION

➡ **Rate your self talk** on a scale of 1-10

1 = negative self talk, beating myself up over a mistake or swearing loudly

10 = bouncing back from a mistake, self talk reflects the process, not the result

Write your score: ______ / 10

➡ **3-2-1 Journaling** *(vary your answers for each day)*

3 ways I can **encourage a teammate** today

(pick a different teammate each day this week)

____

____

____

2 ways I can **practice healthy self talk**

(e.g. process oriented vs. result oriented)

____

____

***1 helpful thing** I can tell myself before my next practice or game*

____

➡ **Visualize.** Spend 5 minutes visualizing what you want to accomplish at practice or in your game today. Find a quiet spot, close your eyes and rehearse this intention.

Thoughts drive behavior. The way we behave after a mistake affects our ability to learn and grow from them or our tendency to get stuck thinking about them.

Things I **DO** after I make a mistake.

1. ____________________
2. ____________________
3. ____________________
4. ____________________

ARE THESE

○ ***Helpful*** to my progress

● ***Not so helpful*** to my progress

DAILY RESET – COMMUNICATION

➡ **Rate your self talk** on a scale of 1-10

1 = negative self talk, beating myself up over a mistake or swearing loudly

10 = bouncing back from a mistake, self talk reflects the process, not the result

Write your score: ______ / 10

➡ **3-2-1 Journaling** *(vary your answers for each day)*

3 ways *I can* ***encourage a teammate*** *today*

(pick a different teammate each day this week)

____

____

____

2 ways *I can* ***practice healthy self talk***

(e.g. process oriented vs. result oriented)

____

____

1 helpful thing *I can tell myself before my next practice or game*

____

➡ **Visualize.** Spend 5 minutes visualizing what you want to accomplish at practice or in your game today. Find a quiet spot, close your eyes and rehearse this intention.

RECAP – COMMUNICATION

Look back at Day 18. You wrote down things you tell a teammate after a mistake. Write them down here, but instead of directing those words at someone else, write them as if you are saying them to yourself.

Choose one of the above comments and **write it in ALL CAPS** here:

This is your MANTRA. Say this to yourself after a mistake, on a tough practice day, on a day you feel down or not motivated.

taking

OWNERSHIP

Your practice is your process. How you use your time is up to you. One of the ways we take ownership of our practice is by **PREPARING** yourself physically, mentally and emotionally for your practice. This is not only a skill that will prepare you for your sport, but it will prepare you for a big test or project you have for school, a job interview, a recruiting visit or a tryout for a new team.

DAILY RESET – OWNERSHIP

Rate your pre-practice/pre-game preparation on a scale of 1-10:

1 = I just roll up and see what happens

10 = I am fully prepared to perform and give my best

Write your score: ______ / 10

3-2-1 Journaling

3 things my sport has allowed me to do *that I'm grateful for*

____

____

____

2 songs or quotes *that put me in a great mood*

____

____

1 person I can talk to *before a game that keeps me focused*

____

Visualize. Spend 5 minutes visualizing what you want to accomplish at practice or in your game today. Find a quiet spot, close your eyes and rehearse this intention.

DAY **22**

___/___/___

1: Who are some athletes I ***admire***?

___

___

___

2: Why do I admire these athletes?

___

___

___

3: What characteristics do they have that I'd like to have?

___

___

___

NEXT LEVEL: *Look up a quote from an athlete that inspires you. Write it down where you can see it daily.*

DAILY RESET – OWNERSHIP

➡ **Rate your pre-practice/pre-game preparation** on a scale of 1-10:

1 = I just roll up and see what happens

10 = I am fully prepared to perform and give my best

Write your score: ______ / 10

➡ **3-2-1 Journaling**

3 things my sport has allowed me to do *that I'm grateful for*

____

____

____

2 songs or quotes *that put me in a great mood*

____

____

1 person I can talk to *before a game that keeps me focused*

____

➡ **Visualize.** Spend 5 minutes visualizing what you want to accomplish at practice or in your game today. Find a quiet spot, close your eyes and rehearse this intention.

DAY **23**

___/___/___

Athletes love control! Unfortunately we cannot control everything, but **we can take responsibility**. INSIDE the hand write five (or more) things I CAN TAKE RESPONSIBILITY FOR in practice/games.

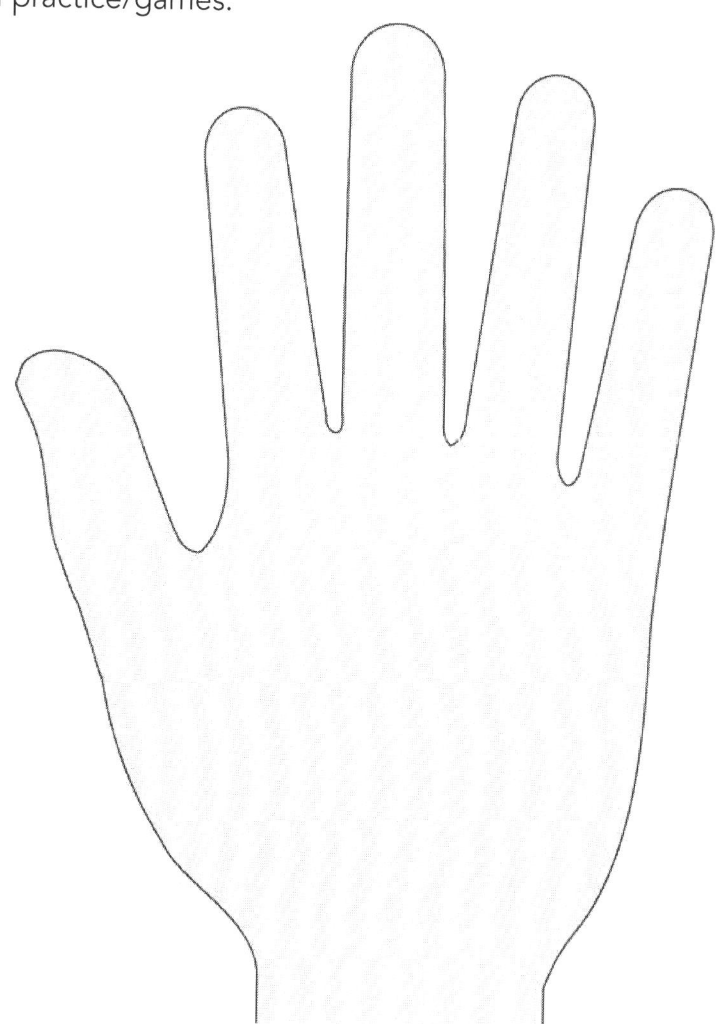

NEXT LEVEL: *Write your favorite ones on your hand for your next practice.*

DAILY RESET – OWNERSHIP

Rate your pre-practice/pre-game preparation on a scale of 1-10:

1 = I just roll up and see what happens

10 = I am fully prepared to perform and give my best

Write your score: ______ / 10

3-2-1 Journaling

3 things my sport has allowed me to do *that I'm grateful for*

____

____

____

2 songs or quotes *that put me in a great mood*

____

____

1 person I can talk to *before a game that keeps me focused*

____

Visualize. Spend 5 minutes visualizing what you want to accomplish at practice or in your game today. Find a quiet spot, close your eyes and rehearse this intention.

DAY **24**

____/____/____

When things feel chaotic, it might be that we are trying to control something **outside our area of responsibility**. OUTSIDE the hand, write five (or more) things I AM NOT RESPONSIBLE FOR in practice/games.

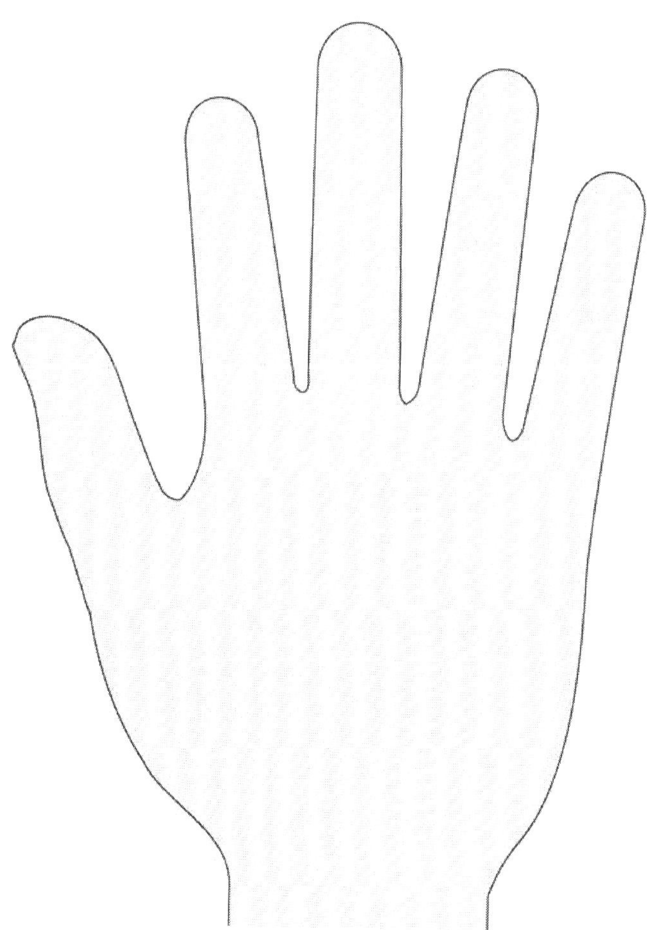

NEXT LEVEL: *Why do you think we wrote these things OUTSIDE of the hand?*

DAILY RESET – OWNERSHIP

Rate your pre-practice/pre-game preparation on a scale of 1-10:

1 = I just roll up and see what happens

10 = I am fully prepared to perform and give my best

Write your score: ______ / 10

3-2-1 Journaling

3 things my sport has allowed me to do *that I'm grateful for*

____

____

____

2 songs or quotes *that put me in a great mood*

____

____

1 person I can talk to *before a game that keeps me focused*

____

Visualize. Spend 5 minutes visualizing what you want to accomplish at practice or in your game today. Find a quiet spot, close your eyes and rehearse this intention.

DAY **25**

___/___/___

You cannot be responsible for both sides of the scoreboard. The highest performers **take ownership** of their inner scoreboard and focus on what they are responsible for and who they are responsible to.

In the **HOME** box, write your team name, team motto and favorite part of being on this team.

In the **AWAY** box, write two things you do to prepare for an AWAY contest or performance.

HOME	AWAY

DAILY RESET – OWNERSHIP

➡ **Rate your pre-practice/pre-game preparation** on a scale of 1-10:

1 = I just roll up and see what happens

10 = I am fully prepared to perform and give my best

Write your score: ______ / 10

➡ **3-2-1 Journaling**

3 things my sport has allowed me to do *that I'm grateful for*

____

____

____

2 songs or quotes *that put me in a great mood*

____

____

1 person I can talk to *before a game that keeps me focused*

____

➡ **Visualize.** Spend 5 minutes visualizing what you want to accomplish at practice or in your game today. Find a quiet spot, close your eyes and rehearse this intention.

DAY 26

___/___/___

When we **take responsibility** over our practice time and our performance in games, we'll begin to see small improvements every time we step on the playing field. One way we can own our practice is writing down and applying the feedback our coaches give us.

List some feedback your coach has given you in the last week or month. Be as specific as possible and see if you can remember the cues they have said, not just general terms:

___

___

___

Have you worked **intentionally** in training to apply these things?

- O yes
- O no
- O I've tried and it's still hard to apply
- O I don't always understand what my coach means

If you answered yes to the last two, it might take a quick conversation or question to clarify what they are asking you to do. Application of skill is different for each athlete and sometimes feedback/cues work differently for different athletes.

DAILY RESET – OWNERSHIP

➡ **Rate your pre-practice/pre-game preparation** on a scale of 1-10:

1 = I just roll up and see what happens

10 = I am fully prepared to perform and give my best

Write your score: ______ / 10

➡ **3-2-1 Journaling**

3 things my sport has allowed me to do *that I'm grateful for*

____

____

____

2 songs or quotes *that put me in a great mood*

____

____

1 person I can talk to *before a game that keeps me focused*

____

➡ **Visualize.** Spend 5 minutes visualizing what you want to accomplish at practice or in your game today. Find a quiet spot, close your eyes and rehearse this intention.

DAY **27**

____/____/____

Perhaps the best way to take ownership of your athletic experience is to understand **WHY** you play your sport. Your **WHY** is rooted in your value systems. Whether you are aware of it or not, you make decisions every day based on your value system. If you know what those values are, you can focus and execute on them daily. If you do not, you will adopt values from social media, your peers, or whomever you decide to follow that particular day. **Circle** some of the values that are most important to you:

FAITH
INTENTIONALITY
DETERMINATIOAN
PERSEVERANCE
WORK ETHIC
JOYFULNESS
FUN
GRATITUDE
ENTHUSIASM
LEARNING

REPUTATION
KNOWLEDGE
GROWTH
HONOR
GRACE
TRUST
INTEGRITY
TEAMWORK
ENJOYMENT
IDENTITY

LOYALTY
DEPENDABILITY
ACHIEVEMENT
AUTHENTICITY
COMMITMENT
FAME
FRIENDSHIPS
POPULARITY
STABILITY
WEALTH

add your own: ________________________________

DAILY RESET – OWNERSHIP

Rate your pre-practice/pre-game preparation on a scale of 1-10:

1 = I just roll up and see what happens

10 = I am fully prepared to perform and give my best

Write your score: ______ / 10

3-2-1 Journaling

3 things my sport has allowed me to do *that I'm grateful for*

____

____

____

2 songs or quotes *that put me in a great mood*

____

____

1 person I can talk to *before a game that keeps me focused*

____

Visualize. Spend 5 minutes visualizing what you want to accomplish at practice or in your game today. Find a quiet spot, close your eyes and rehearse this intention.

DAY **28**

____/____/____

RECAP – OWNERSHIP

Write down **3 reasons WHY** you play your sport:

Write down **three FEARS** you have about playing your sport:

As mentioned on Day 27, our ***WHY*** is rooted in our value system (you circled several that are important to you). Our ***FEARS*** on the other hand are often rooted in shame or guilt. When we ignore our fears, they can become stumbling blocks to performing our best. Though many think otherwise, sharing your fears is NOT a weakness - it's a ***super power***.

Fill in the following equation with **>** or **<**

My WHY is ________ **My FEAR**

POST-GAME HUDDLE

___/___/___

Now that you've completed your 30 days of journaling, re-rate yourself for each question using the scale below. Did any of your scores change? If so, what and why?

1	2	3	4	5
needs work	*meh*	*its fine*	*good*	*great!*

Rate your attitude as an athlete. ________

Rate your effort as an athlete. ________

Rate your openness to feedback. ________

Rate your application of feedback. ________

Rate your openness to ask questions. ________

Rate your pre-practice physical preparation. ________

Rate your pre-game physical preparation. ________

Rate your pre-practice mental preparation. ________

Rate your pre-game mental preparation. ________

Rate your openness to learn something new. ________

Rate your overall performance as an athlete. ________

Information for this appendix has been compiled and created as a source for client education in a clinical setting and may contain research and references from "Social Psychology" by David G Myers & Jean M Twenge.

This appendix is not a diagnostic tool. If you or someone you know have a life threatening situation or need immediate medical help, call your doctor or dial 911.

APPENDIX A

DEPRESSION

What are the symptoms of depression?

- Depressed mood or sadness most of the time
- Lack of energy
- Inability to enjoy things that used to bring pleasure
- Withdrawal from friends and family
- Irritability, anger, or anxiety
- Inability to concentrate
- Significant weight loss or gain
- Significant change in sleep patterns (inability to fall asleep, stay asleep, or get up in the morning)
- Feelings of guilt or worthlessness
- Aches and pains (with no known medical cause)
- Pessimism and indifference (not caring about anything in the present or future)
- Thoughts of death or suicide

When someone has five or more of these symptoms more often than not for two weeks or longer, that person is probably depressed.

APPENDIX A

How is depression different from regular sadness?

Everyone has some ups and downs, and sadness is a natural emotion. The normal stresses of life can lead anyone to feel sad every once in a while. Things like an argument with a friend or spouse, loss of a job, life transitions such as moving or getting a new job or starting a new school, not being chosen for a team, or a best friend moving out of town can lead to feelings of sadness, disappointment, or grief. These reactions are usually brief and go away with a little time and care.

Depression is more than occasionally feeling blue, sad, or down in the dumps, though. Depression is a strong mood involving sadness, discouragement, despair, or hopelessness that lasts for an extended period of time. It interferes with a person's ability to participate in normal activities.

Depression affects a person's thoughts, outlook, and behavior as well as mood. In addition to a depressed mood, a person with depression may feel tired, irritable, and notice changes in appetite. When someone has depression, it can cloud everything. The world looks bleak and the person's thoughts reflect that hopelessness. Depression tends to create negative and self-critical thoughts. Because of feelings of sadness and low energy, those with depression may pull away from those around them or from activities they once enjoyed. This usually makes them feel more lonely and isolated, worsening their condition. Depression can be mild or severe. At its worst, depression can create such feelings of despair that a person contemplates suicide.

APPENDIX **A**

Why does one become depressed?

There is no single cause for depression. Many factors play a role including genetics, life events, family and social environment and medical conditions.

Genetics: Research shows that some individuals inherit genes that make it more likely for them to get depressed. However, not everyone who has the genetic makeup for depression becomes depressed, and many who have no family history of depression have the condition.

Life Events: The death of a family member, friend, or pet can sometimes go beyond normal grief and lead to depression. Other difficult life events, such as when parents divorce, separate, or remarry, can trigger depression. Even events like moving or changing schools can be emotionally challenging enough that a person becomes depressed.

Family and Social Environment: A negative, stressful, or unhappy family atmosphere can have a negative effect on one's self-esteem and lead to depression. This can also include high-stress living situations such as poverty, homelessness, or violence. Substance abuse could cause chemical changes in the brain that negatively impact mood. The damaging social and personal consequences of substance abuse can also lead to depression.

Medical Conditions: Certain medical conditions can affect hormone balance and therefore lead to depression. When these medical conditions are diagnosed and treated by a doctor, the depression usually disappears. For some, undiagnosed learning disabilities might block school, work or relationship success, hormonal changes might affect mood, or physical illnesses might present challenges or setbacks.

How do I get help?

Depression is one of the most common emotional problems around the world. The good news is that it's also one of the most treatable conditions. Those who get help for their depression have a better quality of life and enjoy themselves in ways that they weren't able to before.

Treatment for depression can include psychotherapy, medication, or a combination of both. Psychotherapy with a mental health professional is very effective in treating depression. Therapy sessions can help one understand more about why they feel depressed and learn ways to combat it. Sometimes, doctors prescribe medicine for a patient with depression. It can take a few weeks before that person feels the medicine working. Because every person's brain is different, what works well for one person might not work for another.

Everyone can benefit from mood-boosting activities like exercise, yoga, dance, journaling, or art. It can also help to keep busy no matter how tired you feel.

Those who are depressed shouldn't wait around hoping it will go away on its own; depression can be effectively treated. Others may need to step in if someone seems severely depressed and isn't getting help.

APPENDIX A

Many find that it helps to open up to others including friends, family or other individuals they trust. Simply saying, "I've been feeling really down lately and I think I'm depressed," can be a good way to begin the discussion. Ask to arrange an appointment with a therapist. For teens, if a parent or family member can't help, turn to a school counselor, best friend, or a helpline.

APPENDIX **B**

ANXIETY

Introduction to Anxiety

Generalized Anxiety Disorder or GAD is characterized by excessive, exaggerated anxiety about everyday life events. People with symptoms of GAD tend to always expect disaster and can't stop worrying about health, money, family, work, or school. These worries are often unrealistic or out of proportion for the situation. Daily life becomes a constant state of unease, fear, and dread. Eventually, the anxiety so dominates the person's thinking that it interferes with daily functioning.

What is anxiety?

Anxiety is a natural human reaction that serves an important basic survival function. It acts as an alarm system that is activated whenever a person perceives danger. When the body reacts to a potential threat, a person feels physical sensations of anxiety: a faster heartbeat and breath rate, tensed muscles, sweaty palms, nausea, and trembling hands or legs. These sensations are part of the body's fight-flight response, which is caused by a rush of adrenaline and other chemicals. This reaction prepares the body to make a quick decision to either stay and fight that threat or try to escape from it (fight or flight). It takes a few seconds longer for the thinking part of the brain (the cortex) to process the situation and evaluate whether the threat is real, and if it is, how to handle it. If the cortex sends the all-clear signal, the fight-flight response is deactivated and the nervous system can relax. If the brain reasons that a threat might last, feelings of anxiety and the physical symptoms listed above may linger, keeping the person alert.

What are the symptoms of generalized anxiety disorder?

GAD affects the way a person thinks, but the anxiety can lead to physical symptoms as well. Symptoms of GAD include:

- Excessive, ongoing worry and tension
- An unrealistic view of problems
- Restlessness or a feeling of being "edgy"
- Irritability
- Muscle tension
- Headaches
- Sweating
- Difficulty concentrating
- Nausea
- The need to go to the bathroom frequently
- Tiredness
- Trouble falling or staying asleep
- Trembling
- Being easily startled
- Other anxiety disorders (such as panic disorder, obsessive-compulsive disorder and phobias)

- Depression
- Drug/alcohol abuse

What causes generalized anxiety disorder?

Although the exact cause of GAD is not known, a number of factors, including genetics, brain chemistry, and environmental stressors appear to contribute to its development.

Genetics: Some research suggests that family history plays a part in increasing the likelihood that a person will develop GAD. This means that the tendency to develop GAD may be passed on in families.

Brain chemistry: GAD has been associated with abnormal levels of certain neurotransmitters in the brain. Neurotransmitters are special chemical messengers that help move information between nerve cells. If the neurotransmitters are out of balance, messages cannot travel through the brain properly. This can alter the way the brain reacts in certain situations, leading to anxiety.

Environmental factors: Trauma and stressful events, such as abuse, the death of a loved one, divorce, or changing jobs or schools may lead to GAD. The use of and withdrawal from addictive substances, including alcohol, caffeine, and nicotine, could also worsen anxiety.

How are anxiety disorders treated?

Anxiety disorders can be treated by both mental health professionals and therapists. A therapist can look at the symptoms someone is dealing with, diagnose the specific anxiety disorder, and create a plan to help the person get relief.

A particular type of talk therapy called cognitive-behavior therapy (CBT) is often used. In CBT, a person learns new ways to think and act in situations that can cause anxiety, and to manage and deal with stress. The therapist provides support and guidance and teaches new coping skills such as relaxation techniques or breathing exercises. Sometimes, but not always, medication is used as part of the treatment for anxiety.

How common is generalized anxiety disorder?

About 4 million American adults suffer from GAD during the course of a year. It most often begins in childhood or adolescence, but can begin in adulthood. It is more common in women than in men.

APPENDIX **C**

ADDITIONAL RESOURCES

HOW TO WIN THE NIGHT

Here are our go to's if you are struggling to fall asleep or stay asleep.

Setting yourself up for a good night's rest:

- Create a nightly routine (taking a shower or bath, put on soft music, dim the lights).
- Start the process of preparing for sleep an hour before.
- Go to bed the same time every night.
- Turn off all electronics and/or put the phone face down.

Trouble falling asleep or going back to sleep:

- Reflect on your blessings and what you are grateful for.
- Count backwards from 100.
- Have a notepad next to your bed to write down any pending to do's or thoughts.
- Relax your body by telling your body to go to sleep, starting with your toes and going up to your head.
- After 30 minutes of not being able to fall asleep, get up and do something and then return to your bed.

SUICIDE IDEATION

If you are having suicidal thoughts connect with someone as soon as possible, whether that be a professional, a family member, a friend, or a significant other. Tell them what you are thinking and feeling. Call the suicide hotline 1-800-784-2433 for additional support. For the next 24 hours do not be alone. If you have thoughts, a plan, and means of harming yourself dial 911 or go to your local hospital immediately.

PANIC/ANXIETY ATTACK

Choose one or all of the following, whatever works best for you:

- **Squeeze ice or hold a cold drink.**
  IMPORTANCE: This cools down your CNS (Central Nervous System) and redirects your thoughts onto the coldness of the ice instead of focusing on your anxious thoughts
- **Breathe in through your nose and blow out through pierced lips to maximize your oxygen levels.**
  IMPORTANCE: Your lungs trap oxygen during the time of an attack and this helps you get your oxygen out while at the same time maximizing the oxygen levels in your body.

- **Get outside. Go for a walk and as you walk shift your eyes from left to right.**
  IMPORTANCE: This gets your body moving and back in control of your body. Fresh air is a good change of environment. When you move your eyes from left to right it brings tranquility to the brain.
- **Say the following mantra over and over again, "God is in control, I am okay. I am okay, God is in control."**
  IMPORTANCE: This gets your mind focused off yourself and gives you positive self-talk.
- **Practice grounding exercises using your five senses.** What do you hear, see, smell, taste, or feel around you?
  IMPORTANCE: Activating your five senses will help bring you into the here and now.

COPING SKILLS AND DEFENSIVE MECHANISMS

Defense Mechanisms: Unhealthy ways we respond to our thoughts and emotions.

Coping Skills: Healthy ways we respond to our thoughts and emotions.

DISTRACTIONS

Distractions are people, places or activities that prevent us from giving full attention to something or someone else. When they keep us from getting something done or meeting a goal, distractions are not helpful. When we need a mini-vacation from work, play or from a stressful situation, distractions can be a helpful way to reset our focus. So, how do we choose?

HEALTHY COPING

A coping mechanism is something we do to tolerate or minimize stress or unwanted emotions. Healthy coping may include exercise, eating nutritious foods, spending time with friends or loved ones, journaling, being in nature, resting, meditating, listneing to music, etc. Healthy coping will bring us CLOSER in relationship with ourselves or others. Can you think of some other healthy coping strategtes?

UNHEALTHY COPING

Unhealthy coping PUSHES US AWAY from relationship with ourself or others. Unhealthy coping examples are alcohol or drug abuse, toxic relationships or friendships, abusive relationships, comparing on social media, controlling or blaming others. It can be a substance, a person or a behavior.

NUMBING OUT OR SELF-MEDICATING

If unhealthy coping pushes us away, numbing out and self-medicating ISOLATE US from ourselves or others. These are behaviors, people or substances designed to numb feelings. The problem is when you numb out the unwanted feelings, you also numb out the good ones you need too - leading to further isolation.

HEALTHY COPING BREEDS CONNECTION

Connecting with others and sharing our thoughts and feelings might be the best way to cope and connect. However, when we cannot physicaly connect with others, it's important we still find healthy ways to connect with our own process, emotions and thoughts.

APPENDIX **D**

WHERE IN YOUR BODY

IS YOUR STRESS?

Created by: Priscilla Tallman, MS Clinical Psychology
www.spikedr.com

Notes

Notes

Thank you for completing the **30 Day Champions Journal**! We hope you were able to see the value of daily journaling as a habit and continue the practice through-out your athletic journey. Journaling is part of becoming self-aware as an athlete. Self-awareness helps us see our blind spots and allows us to move forward in strength and power. When we do not acknowledge areas where we get stuck or where we feel alone as athletes, it affects our performance on the field as well as friendships and relationships off the field. Sports is likely a big part of your life, but it's not the only part of your life. We appreciate your willingness to grow and learn with us!

Priscilla Tallman MS, Clinical Psychology

Joe Jardine, MFT

"My favorite part of working through the journal was knowing I had something to go to when I was feeling discouraged about my injury."

–Collegiate Baseball player about the
30 Day Return to Play Journal

"Using the journal is a great way to remind yourself of who you are as an athlete. It keeps you honest with your progress but also brings you back in when you start to doubt yourself,"

–Collegiate Baseball player about the
30 Day Return to Play Journal

"This has been a valuable resource for my teams for two seasons. Not only does it provide a shared language and allow for team discussion, it teaches the essence of learning sports. I recommend this journal for any team or athlete wanting to understand the total picture of athletics"

–Kelly O'Connor, Youth and Club Volleyball Coach

"During the calls with Priscilla, I learned to better embrace tension by being curious about it, rather than ignoring it. I also learned to focus on my values regardless of what external factors I face. I came away from it much more confident in myself and my ability to navigate the challenges that undoubtedly arise in sport and in life."

–Alexis Conway, Professional Volleyball Player

MORE BOOKS BY AUTHOR PRISCILLA TALLMAN

The 30 Day Return to Play Journal is a mindset tool and resource for your athlete to navigate the mental aspect of returning to play after an injury.

Priscilla Tallman is a Mindset and Performance Coach who trains teams, coaches, businesses and individual athletes on mindset and mental skills by combining her playing and coaching experience as well as her educational background in psychology. Tallman's athletic career includes First Team All-America honors and First Team All-SEC honors all four years at the University of Georgia as a volleyball student-athlete including Freshman of the year and Player of the year. Tallman also played two tours with the USA National Team and a year of professional volleyball in Geneva, Switzerland. In 2006, she was inducted into the University of Georgia's prestigious Circle of Honor.

Tallman has an undergraduate degree in Psychology and a Master of Science Degree in Clinical Psychology from Vanguard University. She is active as a coach in youth sports, local club sports and has coached beach volleyball at the high school, club and collegiate levels (NCAA, PAC-12 and NAIA, GSAC). Her passion and work is to raise, train and teach athletes mindset skills that will give them an edge in their sport and healthy habits for life.

Joe Jardine is a performance mindset coach for elite athletes and coaches in the NFL and NCAA. He is privileged to work with athletes and coaches from several organizations including the Dallas Cowboys, Detroit Lions, LA Rams, USC, CAL, UCLA, Northwestern, Notre Dame and more. Joe has a private practice in Orange County California and is a Sports Psychology Professor at Vanguard University.